PEOPLE AT
THE CENTER OF

THE WAR OF 1812

By ROB EDELMAN
AND AUDREY KUPFERBERG

BLACKBIRCH PRESS

An imprint of Thomson Gale, a part of The Thomson Corporation

THOMSON

GALE

Detroit • New York • San Francisco • San Diego • New Haven, Conn.
Waterville, Maine • London • Munich

For more information, contact
Blackbirch Press
27500 Drake Rd.
Farmington Hills, MI 48331-3535
Or you can visit our Internet site at http://www.gale.com

LIBRARY OF CONGRESS CATALOGING-IN-PUBLICATION DATA

Edelman, Rob.
    The War of 1812 / by Rob Edelman and Audrey Kupferberg.
        p. cm. — (People at the center of)
Includes bibliographical references and index.
    ISBN 1-56711-926-3 (hardcover : alk. paper)
    1. United States—History—War of 1812—Juvenile literature. I. Kupferberg, Audrey E.
II. Title. III. Series.
    E354.E33 2005
    973.5'2—dc22

                                                                    2004016944

Printed in the United States of America

CONTENTS

PEOPLE AT
THE CENTER OF

THE WAR OF 1812

The War of 1812 (1812–1815) was the second major confrontation between the United States and Britain after the Revolutionary War (1775–1783). The two nations experienced problems for years before they actually faced off in battle. In the early nineteenth century, the British were fighting the French in the Napoleonic Wars (1803–1815). When their navy ran short of manpower, they began attacking U.S. ships and forcing American sailors into service. The resulting crisis peaked in June 1807, when the British warship *Leopard* attacked the USS *Chesapeake*, an American frigate, three miles off the coast of Norfolk, Virginia. During the assault, three American sailors died, and eighteen were wounded.

An infuriated Thomas Jefferson, the U.S. president, ordered that British ships not be allowed into American ports. That December, the U.S. Congress passed the Embargo Act, which prohibited American firms from transacting business with foreign countries and American ships from venturing onto the high seas. The act was intended to prevent attacks on U.S. ships. However, it served only to ravage New England businesses, which relied on foreign trade to sell their products, and wreck the American economy. It was repealed in 1809, just before James Madison replaced Jefferson in the White House.

When Madison began his presidency, a war with Britain seemed unavoidable. The new chief executive, however, wished to forestall the crisis. In an attempt to do so, he imposed a new trade embargo on the British. This embargo, however, only perpetuated the economic woes caused by the earlier Embargo Act and did nothing to alleviate the seizing of U.S. ships. Many powerful Americans, especially the "War Hawks," a group of congressmen who were clamoring for battle, criticized the president's actions as ineffective. They also saw war as a means for allowing the United States to expand its border into Canada, which then was controlled by the

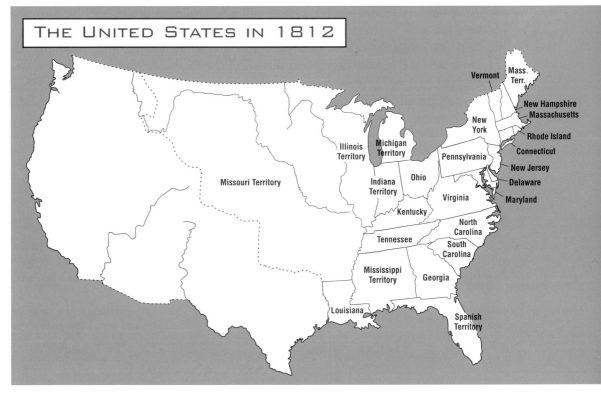

THE UNITED STATES IN 1812

Vermont
Mass. Terr.
New Hampshire
Massachusetts
New York
Rhode Island
Connecticut
New Jersey
Delaware
Maryland
Illinois Territory
Michigan Territory
Pennsylvania
Missouri Territory
Indiana Territory
Ohio
Virginia
Kentucky
North Carolina
Tennessee
South Carolina
Mississippi Territory
Georgia
Louisiana
Spanish Territory

British. Madison finally gave in to the War Hawks and asked Congress for a declaration of war, which he signed on June 18, 1812.

Not all Americans were as pro-war as the War Hawks. Some in Congress, most prominently John Randolph of Virginia, and several state leaders, including Governor Caleb Strong of Massachusetts, condemned the war.

The first major encounter between the Americans and British took place in the Michigan Territory, which bordered Canada. In July 1812, U.S. brigadier general William Hull led his army across the Detroit River into Canada to attack the British and their Canadian and Indian collaborators. Hull's miscalculations resulted in retreat and defeat, with the British taking control of the territory. Their victory led to a decrease in confidence among the entire U.S. military.

The tide of the war in fact did not favor the United States for over a year, until September 1813. At that time, Oliver Hazard Perry, a U.S. Navy commander, decisively defeated the British on Lake Erie, strategically bordered by southeastern Canada, western New York, northwestern Pennsylvania, northern Ohio, and the Michigan Territory. Perry's conquest gave the United States a solid foothold in the region and permitted William Henry Harrison, supreme commander of U.S. forces in the northwest, to move his army into Upper Canada.

As the fighting progressed, the British still won a number of noteworthy battles. Most significantly, in August 1814, their armies landed on the Atlantic coast, beat the Americans at the Battle of Bladensburg in Maryland, and attacked Washington, D.C. Madison and his cabinet fled the city, and the British set fire to the White House and Capitol. Their success was short-lived, however, as they were overpowered by the Americans as they advanced on Fort McHenry in Baltimore. It was during this battle that Francis Scott Key, a Washington, D.C., attorney, authored a poem that eventually became known as "The Star-Spangled Banner." The British suffered another serious blow when they were defeated at Plattsburgh, near the Canadian border in upstate New York.

Meanwhile, British and American negotiators were meeting in Ghent, a city in Belgium, to discuss and potentially agree upon an end to the hostilities. On Christmas Eve, 1814, both sides signed the Treaty of Ghent, which officially ended the War of 1812. Ironically, the British attacks on U.S. ships, conscription of U.S. seamen, and subsequent U.S. trade policies—all direct causes of the war—were not mentioned in the treaty. The Americans and British merely consented to return to

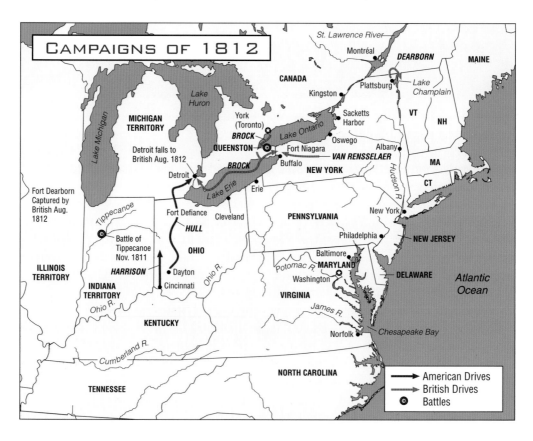

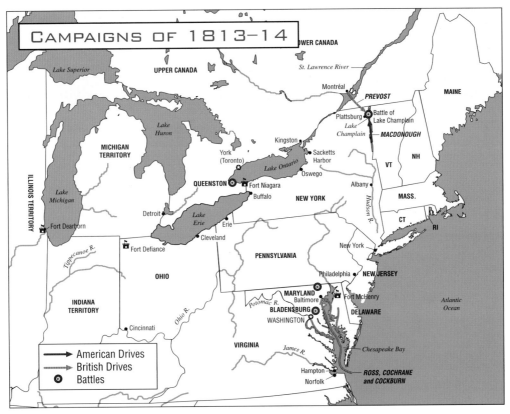

CAMPAIGNS OF 1813-14

American Drives
British Drives
Battles

the same North American boundaries that existed before the war.

Despite the Treaty of Ghent, the final battle of the War of 1812 was yet to be fought. During the latter months of 1814, the British were planning a major attack on the American South. They had chosen New Orleans as their port of entry. Neither the Americans nor the British in the region had received word that the war had ended when the British mounted an all-out offensive on January 8, 1815. They were soundly defeated, suffering over two thousand casualties, while the Americans, under Major General Andrew Jackson, lost but thirteen. Jackson's triumph at New Orleans made him the war's most celebrated military hero. Playing a major role in the victory was Jean Laffite, a French-born pirate who sided with the United States after being courted by the British.

Neither the British nor the Americans were clear-cut victors in the War of 1812. Nonetheless, the standoff proved that the recently liberated colonies were more than capable of asserting and defending themselves. The individual military triumphs encouraged national self-assurance and helped further expansion across the North American continent.

THOMAS JEFFERSON

PRESIDENT WHOSE POLICIES LAID GROUNDWORK FOR THE WAR

Thomas Jefferson was born at Shadwell in Albemarle County, Virginia, in 1743. He attended the College of William and Mary in Williamsburg, worked as a lawyer, was a member of the Virginia House of Burgesses (the first popularly elected legislature in North America), and became a delegate to the Second Continental Congress. In 1776, he authored most of the Declaration of Independence. He served as the governor of Virginia, then as a minister to France, and later as secretary of state under President George Washington. In 1800, he became the third U.S. president.

The USS Chesapeake *battles the British ship* HMS Leopard *during the War of 1812.*

Jefferson was reelected in 1804. Early in his second term, he insisted that the United States remain neutral in the Napoleonic Wars, which pitted England against France. This policy proved difficult to uphold. Because their navy lacked manpower, the British began attacking American ships and conscripting American sailors. Despite this development, Jefferson remained reluctant to declare war against England.

In June 1807, the *Leopard*, a British warship, requested permission to board the USS *Chesapeake*, an American frigate. After the *Chesapeake* captain refused, the *Leopard* launched an attack. Three U.S. seamen died, and eighteen were wounded. Jefferson was outraged. After calling an emergency cabinet meeting, he issued a proclamation ordering the closing of all U.S. ports to British ships. He also urged the U.S. Congress to approve the Embargo Act, which was passed in December 1807. This law forbade American ships from crossing the high seas and American businesses from trading with foreign countries.

Jefferson's strategy, intended to protect American Shipping, proved counterproductive. All it accomplished was the devastation of both New England businesses and the American economy, which relied heavily on foreign trade. The act was repealed in March 1809, days before Jefferson left office. Overall, Jefferson's foreign

Angered by British attacks on American ships, Thomas Jefferson ordered that no British ships be allowed into U.S. ports.

policy initiatives—most significantly, those in response to British aggression against American ships—laid the groundwork for the War of 1812.

After leaving office, Jefferson settled in Monticello, Virginia, his family estate. His vast collection of books, which he sold to the federal government, served as the foundation of the Library of Congress. He also founded the University of Virginia. He died in 1826.

JAMES MADISON

PRESIDENT WHO LED U.S. INTO WAR

James Madison was born in Port Conway, Virginia, in 1751. He graduated from the College of New Jersey (Princeton University), assisted in the writing of Virginia's state constitution, and served in the Continental Congress and Virginia Assembly. His input into the creation of the U.S. Constitution earned him the nickname "Father of the Constitution." He also represented Virginia in the U.S. Congress, helped organize the Republican Party, and was secretary of state under President Thomas Jefferson.

Madison was the fourth U.S. president, following Jefferson into office and serving two terms after being elected in 1808. A war with England seemed a certainty when he entered office, but he was determined to maintain peace. He knew that a conflict would create a need for the imposition of a high national tax and for the establishment of a permanent standing army—both of which he hoped to avoid—as well as endanger the lives and property of U.S. citizens. Instead of fighting the British, Madison preferred to focus on reestablishing the U.S. commercial trade that had been outlawed by the recently repealed Embargo Act.

After having his ship seized, an American sailor is forced to serve in the British navy.

Subsequent maneuvering on the part of Madison with regard to U.S. trade policy, however, failed to halt the seizing of U.S. ships. To many Americans, and particularly the congressional War Hawks who were anxious to face the British in battle, Madison's foreign policy decisions were inadequate. Also at issue was England's control of Canada. The War Hawks saw a confrontation with England as an excuse to seize control of America's northerly neighbor. Madison finally relented and requested that Congress declare war. On June 18, 1812, he signed a declaration of war against England. He was the U.S. president throughout the war.

After leaving office in 1817, Madison withdrew to Montpelier, his Virginia plantation, and advised his successor, James Monroe, on foreign policy matters. He also became rector of the University of Virginia, and he died in 1836.

Though James Madison wanted peace, congressional War Hawks pressured him to declare war on England.

HENRY CLAY

Henry Clay was born in Hanover County, Virginia, in 1777. He worked as a court clerk and became a lawyer, and then earned renown as a brilliant criminal defense attorney in Lexington, Kentucky. He served in the Kentucky state legislature and, briefly, the U.S. Senate. He was elected to the U.S. House of Representatives in 1810.

Clay's reputation led to his being chosen Speaker of the House. He and fellow congressmen John C. Calhoun of South Carolina and Felix Grundy of Tennessee all came into office between 1810 and 1811. They became known as the "War Hawks" because of their firm commitment to fighting a war with England, which they felt was necessary and inevitable.

Clay, Calhoun, and Grundy believed that the future of the United States depended upon westward expansion. A war with England, from their perspective, would eliminate any obstruction on the part of the British to the American settlement of the West. Such a conflict might even allow the United States to annex Canada, which was controlled by the British.

The War Hawks also wished to take over Florida, which was under Spanish domain. England was allied with Spain, and a victory over England surely would increase the likelihood that Spain would cede Florida to the United States (which it did, in 1819). On more general terms, the War Hawks felt that a confrontation with England would increase the new nation's international prestige and boost pride and patriotism among Americans. Ultimately, Clay and the other War Hawks were a major force in stirring up pro-war sentiment, urging U.S. military preparedness, and pressuring President James Madison to declare war against the British.

By 1814, two years into the fighting, it appeared that England might be willing to negotiate a peace. Deliberations began in Ghent, Belgium, and Madison chose Clay as one of the chief U.S. negotiators.

Clay remained Speaker of the House through 1820 and also held the position from 1823 to 1825. He served as secretary of state under President John Quincy Adams and became a U.S. senator. On five occasions, he unsuccessfully ran for president. He died in 1852.

Henry Clay was the leader of the War Hawk faction, which wanted war with England.

Speaker of the House Henry Clay addresses the Senate. Clay believed strongly in westward expansion.

John Randolph was born in Prince George County, Virginia, in 1773. He briefly studied law and was elected to the U.S. House of Representatives in 1799.

Randolph often championed minority political causes and was famed as a supporter of states' rights and individual freedom. He vehemently opposed going to war with Britain and dubbed fellow congressmen Henry Clay, John C. Calhoun, and Felix Grundy the "War Hawks" because of their fierce support for such a conflict.

Randolph believed that the War Hawks primarily wanted a showdown with England because they wished the United States to expand its boundaries westward and into Canada. He, in turn, felt that each U.S. state should focus primarily on its own issues and interests. Furthermore, he believed that the United States lacked the military might to defeat Britain. Such a war also would lead to a rebellion among slaves in the United States, who would side with the enemy. He felt that American citizens would rebel against being taxed to raise money to fund the war. He argued that it would be unwise for the United States to clash with the country with which it was most closely linked culturally and historically.

John Randolph (far right) served in the House of Representatives. He opposed war with England.

Randolph's opposition remained staunch even after President James Madison declared war against the British, and it led to the loss of his congressional seat during the 1813 election. However, Randolph's vocal and emphatic antiwar stance stood out against the view of the War Hawks and emphasized the fact that not all those in Congress were anxious to battle the British.

Randolph won back his seat in 1815. He served additional terms in the House, was briefly a U.S. Senator, and died in 1833.

John Randolph remained passionately antiwar even after President Madison declared war on the British, demonstrating that not all in Congress supported the war.

THE WAR OF 1812 17

CALEB STRONG

Caleb Strong was born in Northampton, Massachusetts, in 1745. A Harvard graduate, he became a lawyer and local government official, a delegate to the Massachusetts constitutional convention, and finally a state and U.S. senator. He also was a leading member of the Federalist Party, the first U.S. political party. He was elected governor of Massachusetts in 1800, failed in a reelection bid in 1807, and retook the office in 1812.

In the early 1800s, New England businesspeople were alarmed by the possibility of a war with England. The fighting would prevent them from freely trading with neutral nations, which they believed would leave them in financial shambles. As governor of Massachusetts, Strong represented their interests in spearheading opposition to the war. He urged the Massachusetts citizenry to fast in protest and suggested they voice their condemnation of the conflict at county and town meetings.

The governor felt that he solely was responsible for determining if circumstances existed that required the men of Massachusetts to fight. He believed that none did, despite President James Madison's declaration of war, and refused to send his state militia into combat. While he commanded that the militia remain prepared for battle, in case of a British attack, it would fight for Massachusetts alone and not the entire union. Other New England states also employed this strategy.

Throughout the war, Strong continued to clash with federal authorities. This conflict resulted in the Hartford Convention, during which Federalist Party representatives from Massachusetts, Rhode Island, Vermont, New Hampshire, and Connecticut met and agreed upon seven proposed amendments to the U.S. Constitution that spotlighted their grievances against the federal government. Among the issues they addressed was the manner in which the U.S. Congress could place embargoes, control trade, and declare war. By the time the delegates arrived in Washington, D.C., to present their proposals, the Treaty of Ghent was signed.

After the war, Hartford Convention participants were accused of conspiring to secede from the union, a claim that resulted in the dissolution of the Federalist Party. Strong decided not to run for reelection in 1816. He died in 1819.

Massachusetts governor Caleb Strong opposed the war and refused to send his state troops into combat.

Etched by Albert Rosenthal Phila 1888 after Painting by G. Stuart

WILLIAM HULL

U.S. GENERAL WHO LED FAILED
INVASION OF CANADA

William Hull was born in Derby, Connecticut, in 1753. He attended Yale College, practiced law, fought in the American army during the Revolutionary War, and later became a judge and Massachusetts state senator. In 1805, President Thomas Jefferson named him governor of the new Michigan Territory.

At the start of the War of 1812, Hull was commissioned a brigadier general by President James Madison and assigned to lead U.S. forces in the territory. His mission was to protect the territory as well as launch an attack on the British and their Canadian and Indian allies. Hull assured the U.S. War Department that he could compel the British to abandon their ships on Lake Erie. It was a major miscalculation.

As he surrenders, William Hull hands his sword to British general Isaac Brock.

In July 1812, one month into the war, Hull and approximately two thousand soldiers, mostly Ohio militiamen, arrived at Fort Detroit and crossed the Detroit River into Canada. However, he delayed his attack against the British post at Amherstburg, figuring that the Canadians would refuse to fight. This postponement allowed the British to cut off and isolate the Americans beside the Lake Erie shore and Detroit River and overtake the American post at Mackinac. The British force was led by Isaac Brock, a major general and the governor and military commander of Upper Canada.

Hull's forces retreated to Fort Detroit. Brock, meanwhile, chose to pursue Hull across the border. Even though Brock had less manpower than the Americans, Hull surrendered without firing a shot. His rationale was that he was surrounded by the enemy, unable to communicate with his comrades in arms in Ohio, and lacking sufficient supplies to sustain a lengthy battle.

Hull's inaction resulted in a loss of self-confidence within the entire American military and helped set the tone for the war's early stages. He subsequently was

William Hull mistakenly believed he could attack the British in Canada. Hull's surrender at Fort Detroit demoralized the American military.

court-martialed and found guilty of treason, cowardice, and negligence of duty. He was scheduled to be executed, but Madison commuted the sentence because of Hull's heroism during the Revolutionary War.

Hull was mustered out of the military and returned to his family in Massachusetts. He died in 1825.

OLIVER HAZARD PERRY

COMMANDER WHO DEFEATED BRITISH NAVY ON LAKE ERIE

Oliver Hazard Perry was born in South Kingston (or Kingstown), Rhode Island, in 1785. He spent his early life at sea, enlisting in the U.S. Navy at age fourteen and serving on board ships in the West Indies and Mediterranean.

At the start of the War of 1812, Perry was commanding a flotilla of twelve gunboats anchored at Newport, Virginia. His mission was to defend Newport in the event of a British attack. During the first months of 1813, he was given the more demanding assignment of leading American naval forces on Lake Erie, which was controlled by the British. His initial task was to supervise construction of a fleet of ships at Erie, Pennsylvania, a daunting assignment because of a lack of supplies and manpower. Primarily because of Perry's unflappable determination, the construction was completed by the summer. That September, the new fleet faced off against the British.

Oliver Hazard Perry and his forces triumphed after fighting fiercely at the Battle of Lake Erie.

Initially, a British blockade prevented Perry from maneuvering the *Lawrence* and *Niagara*, his largest ships, over a sandbar and onto the lake. Then the British commander, Robert H. Barclay, inexplicably lifted the blockade, thus allowing Perry access to the lake. Barclay eventually confronted Perry, and their fleets clashed on September 10. While each possessed similar numbers of sailors, the Americans boasted superior firepower. After a furious battle that lasted more than three hours, the Americans emerged victorious. After Barclay's surrender, Perry penned a celebrated, oft-quoted dispatch: "We have met the enemy and they are ours."

Perry's victory enabled the Americans to control Lake Erie and the surrounding region for the rest of the war. It also allowed William Henry Harrison access to a major portion of Upper Canada, which the forces in his command eventually secured.

After the war, Perry continued his U.S. Navy service. He died in 1819 at the age of thirty-four after being stricken with yellow fever.

Oliver Hazard Perry's victory over the British gave America control of Lake Erie, paving the way for invasion of Canada.

WILLIAM HENRY HARRISON

COMMANDER WHO SUCCESSFULLY PURSUED BRITISH INTO CANADA

William Henry Harrison was born in Charles City County, Virginia, in 1773. He attended Virginia's Hampden-Sidney College and the University of Pennsylvania, served in the U.S. Army, and became secretary of the Northwest Territory, the territory's first congressional delegate, and governor of the Indiana Territory.

In August 1812, two months after the United States declared war against Britain, Harrison reentered the military. In the wake of William Hull's surrender of Fort Detroit and the Michigan Territory to the British, Harrison became supreme commander of American forces in the northwest.

The victorious commander William Henry Harrison rides on horseback at the Battle of Tippecanoe.

A series of military miscalculations culminated in an unsuccessful bid to take back the Michigan Territory from the British. Harrison's failure, however, was fleeting. After their defeat at Lake Erie in September 1813, the British retreated eastward into Canada—and Harrison immediately launched an all-out offensive. His forces first captured Malden, a small British community near Fort Detroit, then retook Fort Detroit and immediately advanced into Canada.

In October, Harrison and his troops took the British by surprise in the Battle of the Thames (so named because it was fought on Canada's Thames River). The struggle was brief, and the Americans emerged victorious. Harrison's triumph, added to that of the British defeat at Lake Erie, gave the Americans a permanent foothold in the northeastern United States and Canada.

Harrison resigned from the military before the end of the war. In 1814 and 1815, he led negotiations with northwestern Indian tribes that resulted in the U.S. occupation of Indian lands. He served in the Ohio state senate, the U.S. House of Representatives, and the U.S. Senate, became ambassador to Colombia, and was elected the ninth U.S. president in 1840. He died of pneumonia the following year, one month after taking office.

After recapturing Fort Detroit, William Henry Harrison marched into Canada, giving America control of the northeast.

TECUMSEH

Tecumseh was born in Old Piqua, a Shawnee village in Ohio, in 1768. His mother was said to have been a Creek Indian, and his father was a Shawnee chief. His name may be translated as "Shooting Star" or "Panther Springing Across the Sky." As he reached adulthood, Tecumseh developed into an excellent hunter, warrior, and orator. By 1808, he had become a Shawnee chief.

During the early nineteenth century, American Indian tribes increasingly were becoming fearful of U.S. expansion into the southern and western regions of North America. Tecumseh was deeply concerned about the plight of his fellow Indians, and he refused to participate in any territorial negotiations or treaties with the United States. He even attempted to bring together all midwestern and southern tribes to repel American attempts to take over Indian land. He believed that, if they failed, a massive war between the Americans and Indians would be unavoidable.

Tecumseh also felt that the British in Canada would be allied with the Indians in such a conflict. The British already were supporting his efforts to unite the Indian tribes. Their rationale was that they would require all the military support they could gather in the event of a war with the United States, and Tecumseh would be a powerful ally. Once the War of 1812 began, Tecumseh indeed sided with the British. As a powerful and influential Indian leader, he represented American Indian participation in the war.

The British bestowed on Tecumseh the rank of brigadier general and allowed him to command all Indian fighters. The chief and six hundred of his warriors were instrumental in assisting Isaac Brock, the British military commander of Upper Canada, in his conquest of Fort Detroit and the Michigan Territory. Despite his distrust of the Americans, Tecumseh was merciful in victory and was instrumental in insuring that American soldiers were spared from massacre.

Tecumseh also led his followers into battles at Brownstown, in the Michigan Territory (where he and 24 warriors reportedly overpowered 150 American troops), and at Fort Meigs and Fort Stephenson in Ohio. He was killed in 1813 during the Battle of the Thames.

Tecumseh wanted to form a large union of Indian tribes to block American takeover of Indian lands.

The death of Tecumseh as he and his warriors fight American troops at the Battle of the Thames is shown in this engraving.

Lord Henry Bathurst led the British military effort during the War of 1812. He greatly underestimated the Americans.

LORD HENRY BATHURST

DIRECTED BRITISH WAR EFFORT

Henry Bathurst, Third Earl Bathurst, was born in Gloucestershire, England, in 1762. After serving in the British Parliament, he held numerous government posts, including lord of the British Admiralty, lord of the British Treasury, master of the mint, and president of the British Board of Trade.

At the outset of the War of 1812, Bathurst was appointed secretary of state for war and the colonies. This position made him—more than any other British government official—most directly in charge of his country's military effort in the war.

Initially, his chief concern was Britain's ongoing conflict with France in the Napoleonic Wars. After Napoleon I lost power in 1814, he shifted his focus to the fighting in North America.

By June 1814, Bathurst had come to believe that a sufficient number of British troops were in place in Canada to allow for a major offensive. After ordering the transferral of supplementary troops from Europe to Canada, he directed that the British occupy several islands in Passamaquoddy Bay, located between Maine (which then was a part of Massachusetts) and the Canadian province of New Brunswick. Then he instructed Sir George Prevost, the governor general and head colonial minis-

American victory in the naval battle at New York's Plattsburgh Harbor undermined Bathurst's strategy.

ter of Canada, who commanded British forces in North America, to launch the offensive. Prevost's mission was a multilayered one. It included striking the Americans at Sackett's Harbor and Plattsburgh in upstate New York, wrecking naval outposts on Lakes Erie and Champlain, and retaking Fort Detroit.

Bathurst's strategy was undercut in the fall when the British were defeated at Plattsburgh and Baltimore. Nonetheless, he took an uncompromising position at the Ghent peace talks, contending that Britain be permitted to keep the territories it had won during the war. He finally agreed that territorial rights in North America would remain as they had been before the war.

Bathurst remained secretary of state for war and the colonies through 1827. He died in 1834.

Dolly Madison was a popular hostess and an active member of the social life in Washington, D.C.

DOLLY (DOLLEY) MADISON

Dolly (or Dolley) Madison was born Dorothy (possibly Dorothea) Payne in Guilford, North Carolina, in 1768. At age twenty-one, she married John Todd Jr., a lawyer who died in 1793 during a yellow fever epidemic. Dolly and her surviving son—a second child also perished in the epidemic—moved into the Philadelphia boardinghouse operated by her mother. There, she met James Madison, a Virginia congressman, whom she married in 1794.

Dolly Madison accompanied her husband to Washington, D.C., in 1801, after he was named President Thomas Jefferson's secretary of state. Jefferson was a widower, and Dolly was enlisted to serve as hostess at presidential social events. She became first lady when Madison won the presidency in 1808. By then, Dolly had earned a reputation as a popular and gracious hostess and one of the mainstays of the Washington social whirl.

In August 1814, the British army came ashore on the Atlantic coast, won a victory at the Battle of Bladensburg in Maryland, and advanced on the U.S. capital. While the president and his cabinet fled to Virginia, the first lady chose to remain at the White House to attempt to salvage important presidential papers. She finally left after receiving a message from the president beseeching her to do so, but not before rescuing numerous federal and presidential documents, some White House silverware, and a full-length portrait of George Washington painted by Gilbert Stuart, the renowned U.S. portrait artist. Upon their arrival at the White House barely two hours after Dolly's departure, the British partook in the food and drink that had been laid out for a presidential dinner party. Then they burned the mansion to the ground.

First Lady Dolly Madison rescues important White House documents shortly before the British arrive.

Dolly Madison's decision to remain in Washington and rescue the presidential artifacts distinguished her as a first lady who was more than just a social hostess. It made her a guardian of American history.

After James Madison left the presidency in 1817, he and Dolly retired to Montpelier, the Madison family home in Virginia. After his death in 1836, Dolly returned to Washington, D.C., where she died in 1849.

Francis Scott Key is best known for writing the poem that eventually became "The Star-Spangled Banner," America's national anthem.

FRANCIS SCOTT KEY

Francis Scott Key was born on his family's estate, Terra Rubra, in Frederick (later Carroll) County, Maryland, in 1779. He completed his formal education at St. John's College in Annapolis and soon afterward became a lawyer. He eventually moved to Washington, D.C., where he established himself as a prominent attorney. He also dabbled in writing poetry.

Key was a deeply religious man who initially opposed the War of 1812. In 1814, he altered his stance and joined the District of Columbia militia. That year, the British attacked Washington, D.C. As they retreated, they detained Dr. William Beanes, a prominent physician. Key was asked to negotiate his release. He and Colonel J.S. Skinner, the U.S. military officer charged with the responsibility of brokering prisoner exchanges, traveled to the British fleet in Chesapeake Bay, Maryland, to win the doctor's freedom.

After a successful negotiation, Key found himself on board a U.S. vessel during a nighttime British assault on Fort McHenry in Baltimore. Upon observing the American flag flying over the fort despite the unyielding British attack, he was inspired to compose a poem, which he inscribed on the back of an envelope. In it, he wrote admiringly of the "broad stripes and bright stars" that remained flying "thro' the perilous fight. . . . the rockets' red glare, the bombs bursting in air." In so doing, he immortalized America's perseverance against the British during the War of 1812.

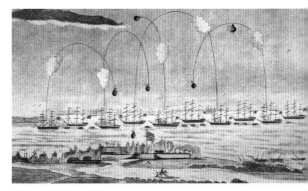

Francis Scott Key wrote a poem describing America's bravery during the War of 1812 after watching the British attack Fort McHenry in Baltimore.

Key's poem was published in the *Baltimore American* a week after it was written. It was titled "Defense of Fort McHenry" and quickly was reprinted in other newspapers. It eventually was set to the melody of "To Anacreon in Heaven," a British drinking song, and initially was sung by Ferdinand Durang, an actor. In 1931, the U.S. Congress enacted legislation that made Key's poem, by then known as "The Star-Spangled Banner," America's national anthem.

After considering a switch in career to the clergy, Key returned to his law practice. He was U.S. attorney for the District of Columbia, served as an emissary for President Andrew Jackson, and died in 1843.

ANDREW JACKSON

COMMANDER WHO DEFEATED BRITISH AT NEW ORLEANS

Andrew Jackson was born in South Carolina's Waxhaw settlement in 1767. At age three he fought in the Revolutionary War and briefly was captured by the British. He later became a lawyer and was a member of the Tennessee constitutional convention, the first U.S. congressman representing Tennessee, a U.S. senator, and a state superior court justice.

During the War of 1812, Jackson earned national recognition when he headed the Tennessee militia. In March 1814, he and his volunteers fought the Creek Indians, who had slaughtered white settlers at Fort Mims, Alabama. Jackson soundly defeated the Creek in the Battle of Horseshoe Bend, in the Mississippi Territory. This victory resulted in the surrender of 23 million acres of Creek territory, which proved to be a gateway for Southern colonization by settlers. Jackson's spirit and determination during this confrontation resulted in his men nicknaming him "Old Hickory."

Jackson then won a commission as a U.S. Army major general and masterminded the defeat of the British in the Battle of New Orleans. In late 1814, rumors were afloat that the British were planning a major invasion of the South by way of New Orleans, and Jackson was directed to impede the assault. He was severely undermanned. Serving under him were a ragtag group consisting of several thousand Tennessee and Kentucky militiamen, French colonists, African slaves, and pirates.

Jackson's strategy was to create a sturdy line of defense outside the city. Following scattered fighting and an artillery barrage, the British launched a major offensive on January 8, 1815. They were decisively defeated. While more than two thousand of their fighters were killed, the Americans reported only thirteen casualties. Ironically, the Battle of New Orleans was fought two weeks after the U.S. and Britain signed the Ghent peace treaty. Both sides were unaware that the war officially had ended. Nevertheless, Jackson's triumph at New Orleans combined with his victory at Horseshoe Bend to make him the foremost hero of the War of 1812.

Andrew Jackson became a national hero after defeating the British at the Battle of New Orleans.

After the war, Jackson became a commander in the U.S. Army, the military governor of the Florida Territory, and a U.S. senator. In 1828, he became the seventh U.S. president, and he won reelection four years later. He retired to the Hermitage, his Tennessee estate, in 1837 and died in 1845.

The British suffered heavy casualties during the Battle of New Orleans, which was fought after the war had officially ended.

Jean Laffite played a principal role in the American victory at New Orleans. After the war, he returned to the buccaneer life.

PIRATE WHO SIDED WITH AMERICANS

Little is certain about the early life of Jean Laffite. Reportedly, he was born in 1780 or 1781 in Bayonne, in southwestern France, and settled in Santo Domingo, on the Caribbean island of Hispaniola, while in his early twenties. He and his brother Pierre soon began operating as pirates and smugglers in and around the Gulf of Mexico and the Caribbean islands, primarily assaulting and looting Spanish ships. In 1810, he and his band put down roots in Barataria Bay, outside New Orleans.

During the fall of 1814, the British were planning a major invasion of the American South. Their port of entry would be New Orleans. Given Laffite's intimate knowledge of the region, his assistance was deemed essential to a British victory. The invaders attempted to pay off the pirate in gold, in exchange for his agreeing to help them. They even recommended him for a British Royal Navy commission.

Despite his lawlessness, Laffite remained a steadfast supporter of France, which long had been embroiled with England in the Napoleonic Wars. He was an admirer of the U.S. Constitution and the freedoms it permitted American citizens. He also wished

Laffite prepares to fire a cannon at the Battle of New Orleans. He and his men fought with the Americans against the British.

to win a U.S. government pardon for his criminal activities. For these reasons, Laffite informed the United States of the British attack plans. He additionally made available to the Americans his men and his weapons and offered input regarding military strategy. He and his pirates fought alongside Andrew Jackson's forces, and they soundly defeated the British. Laffite's decision to assist the Americans before and during the Battle of New Orleans was of major importance in the American victory. For his efforts, he and his crew won pardons from President James Madison.

After the war, Laffite allegedly worked for Spain as a secret envoy. He then resumed his buccaneer ways. Some historians note that he may have settled in southwest Louisiana toward the end of his life. He reportedly died in 1825.

LED THE BRITISH AT THE BATTLE OF NEW ORLEANS

Edward Pakenham was born in Pakenham Hall, County Westmeath, Ireland, in 1778. He began a career in the military and by age seventeen had become a major in the Ulster Light Dragoons. He then served England in numerous military campaigns.

By the start of the War of 1812, Pakenham had risen to the rank of major general. He spent the first years of the conflict in Europe, battling the French in the Napoleonic Wars, and was knighted by King George III in 1813.

General Edward Pakenham is shown dying in the arms of a comrade on the New Orleans battlefield.

The following year, Robert Ross, a British major general, was assigned to direct a British invasion of New Orleans. After leading his army in the capture and burning of Washington, D.C., he was killed during the Battle of Baltimore. Upon Ross's death, Pakenham was named his replacement. He traveled to Jamaica, where he and his subordinates were to plan the invasion. His crossing of the Atlantic was hampered by bad weather, and he arrived in Jamaica after Vice Admiral Alexander Cochrane, a fellow officer, already had left for New Orleans to begin the campaign.

Pakenham landed at the British camp outside New Orleans on December 25, 1814, and took command of the operation. Despite his expertise and leadership, the invasion was doomed from the start. His men had to maneuver artillery over rough terrain. Intelligence information was faulty. The weather was inclement.

After scattered fighting, Pakenham decided to launch a major, two-sided assault on the Americans on January 8. First, the British would attack and capture American artillery positioned on the western bank of the Mississippi. Then, a second attack would be launched from the east. However, Pakenham neglected to wait until the first wave succeeded before authorizing the subsequent assault. This critical error directly led to the British defeat.

During the battle, Pakenham was struck by a cannonball and bumped off his horse. After mounting another, he was hit by one bullet in the throat and another in the chest. He was carried to safety but soon died.

Sir Edward Pakenham's flawed military strategy handed victory to the Americans at the Battle of New Orleans.

CHRONOLOGY

May 1803	Britain declares war on France, starting the Napoleonic Wars, which eventually result in a shortage of manpower on British navy ships.
June 22, 1807	The *Leopard*, a British warship, attacks the USS *Chesapeake*, an American frigate. Three Americans die, and eighteen are wounded.
December 22, 1807	The U.S. Senate passes the Embargo Act.
March 1, 1809	The Embargo Act is repealed.
March 4, 1809	James Madison is inaugurated as the fourth U.S. President.
1810	Henry Clay of Kentucky and John C. Calhoun of South Carolina are elected to the U.S. House of Representatives; fellow War Hawk Felix Grundy of Virginia joins them a year later.
June 1, 1812	Madison requests that the U.S. Congress declare war against the British.
June 18, 1812	Madison signs a declaration of war against England.
July 5, 1812	U.S. brigadier general William Hull arrives at Fort Detroit and prepares to launch an offensive into Canada.
August 16, 1812	Hull surrenders to Isaac Brock, the British governor and military commander of Upper Canada.
September 10, 1813	The U.S. Navy, commanded by Oliver Hazard Perry, wins a decisive victory over the British at Lake Erie.
September 29, 1813	U.S. forces, under William Henry Harrison, supreme commander of American forces in the northwest, retake Fort Detroit from the British.
October 5, 1813	Harrison's forces decisively defeat the British in the Battle of the Thames, during which Tecumseh, the Shawnee chief who supported the British, is killed.

March 27, 1814	The Tennessee militia, under Andrew Jackson, defeats the Creek Indians in the Battle of Horseshoe Bend.
June 1814	Peace negotiations between the U.S. and Britain commence in Ghent, Belgium.
August 1814	The British army comes ashore on the Atlantic coast, wins a victory at the Battle of Bladensburg in Maryland, and advances on Washington, D.C.
August 8, 1814	American and British representatives begin peace negotiations in Ghent, Belgium.
August 24, 1814	Madison and his cabinet flee Washington, D.C., for Virginia as the British army enters the U.S. capital.
September 11, 1814	The Americans defeat the British in the Battle of Plattsburgh.
September 13–14, 1814	Francis Scott Key composes "The Star-Spangled Banner" while observing the unsuccessful British assault on Fort McHenry in Baltimore.
December 15, 1814– January 14, 1815	Federalist Party representatives from Massachusetts, Rhode Island, Vermont, New Hampshire, and Connecticut meet at the Hartford Convention.
December 24, 1814	The U.S. and Britain sign the Treaty of Ghent, ending the War of 1812.
January 8, 1815	The British, unaware that the war has ended, attack Andrew Jackson's forces at New Orleans. They are soundly defeated.
February 16, 1815	The U.S. Senate approves the ratification of the Treaty of Ghent.
February 17, 1815	Madison ratifies the Treaty of Ghent.

FOR FURTHER INFORMATION

BOOKS

Peter I. Bosco, *The War of 1812*. Brookfield, CT: Millbrook Press, 1991.

Miriam Greenblatt, *War of 1812*. New York: Facts On File, 1994.

Albert Marrin, *1812: The War Nobody Won*. New York: Atheneum, 1985.

Milton Meltzer, *Thomas Jefferson: The Revolutionary Aristocrat*. New York: Franklin Watts, 1991.

Don Nardo, *The War of 1812*. San Diego: Lucent, 2000.

Rebecca Stefoff, *Tecumseh and the Shawnee Federation*. New York: Facts On File, 1998.

WEB SITES

War of 1812
www.multied.com/1812/index.html
A history of the war, with links to the major battles.

War of 1812
www.galafilm.com/1812/
A history of the war, serving as a companion to a documentary film about the conflict.

War of 1812
www.army.mil/cmh-pg/books/amh/amh-06.htm
Extracted from *American Military History*, Army Historical Series, issued by the U.S. Army Office of the Chief of Military History.

PICTURE CREDITS

ABOUT THE AUTHOR

Rob Edelman is a writer who lives with his wife Audrey Kupferberg in Amsterdam, New York. He has authored several books on baseball and movie and television personalities, and teaches film history at the University of Alnbany. He enjoys watching old movies and attending baseball games.

INDEX